no particular place to go

Also by Laurie Duggan

Poetry

East: Poems 1970–74 (1976)
[East and Under the Weather (2014)]
Under the Weather (1978)
Adventures in Paradise (1982, 1991)
The Great Divide, Poems 1973–83 (1985)
The Ash Range (1987; 2nd edition, 2005*)
The Epigrams of Martial (1989)
Blue Notes (1990)
The Home Paddock (1991)
Memorials (1996)
New and Selected Poems, 1971–1993 (1996)
Mangroves (2003)
Compared to What: Selected Poems 1971–2003 (2005)*
The Passenger (2006)
Crab & Winkle (2009)*
The Epigrams of Martial (2010)
The Collected Blue Hills (2011)
The Pursuit of Happiness (2012)*
Allotments (2014)*

Cultural history

Ghost Nation (2001)

*Shearsman titles

Laurie Duggan

no particular place to go

Shearsman Books

First published in the United Kingdom in 2017 by
Shearsman Books
50 Westons Hill Drive
Emersons Green
BRISTOL
BS16 7DF

Shearsman Books Ltd Registered Office
30–31 St. James Place, Mangotsfield, Bristol BS16 9JB
(this address not for correspondence)

www.shearsman.com

ISBN 978-1-84861-521-2

Contents

Readers

for Tony Frazer

André Kertész photographed them
hunched over a paper,

seen from above on a rooftop
or below on a fire escape,

shadowed in a park,
or lit up on a bench

knees holding a book,
a cow over this one's shoulder

Afterimages

Peter Lanyon

those quadrilaterals,
hedges, a landing strip
seen through cross-hairs

that line, a strut or cliff edge
a sudden dip or buffet
a broad slash of blue

landscape, suggested once by a Claude glass
might be just this … this … this,
like ornithology: 'for the birds'

*

Frank Auerbach

down Primrose Hill
two lights, feeble in middle ground,
hemmed in by shrubbery

orange visibility vests on a lime coloured oval
a street wet behind glass
pedestrians lit by the glow of phones

the open cigarette packet on the pub table
is a strategy, pencil backwards
on the interlocutor's ear

dusty window panes
haloed by sunlight
bright squares on a bar floor

*

Alexander Calder

ballet shoes point upward
a slight figure, lifted

by a thickset one
the weight of both

an absence, suggested
by continuous line

so the testes become a leg
an elbow becomes a signature

the space enclosed
animate;

across the aisle
Josephine Baker

dances, her shadow
lifeless on the wall

*

Gustave Courbet

The cliffs of Ornans appear
as they do through the gallery window,

the local characters enlarged, a bourgeois presumption
to be bigger than Napoleon (a short man),

to inhabit a large canvas, as though
worthy of the academy.

What made him present himself, greeted on the road
by another figure (engaged perhaps

in mere commerce) offer instead of an epithet
a commonplace?

*

Jacopo Bassano

Light breaks (or fades) over a distant mountain
but the figures in the foreground are too intent

to notice, animals martialled up a ramp in pairs,
eggs collected in a basket. The humans

bundle possessions, sort copper pans, have
no time to view even the rising water.

To the left a monkey holds what looks like
a sceptre – has all sense deserted these people

alive in the cramped space of a jigsaw? All questions
seem to have an answer in this world

but where is the cat's companion?

*

Basil King

The face could be
lunar, its craters

the glint of an eye,
bend sinister of the mouth;

half is in eclipse,
an orange shadow,

the other half glances out
at invisible events,

history maybe, or
just a present

occurring somewhere
behind you;

a glow, or
halo surrounds it

*

Mona Hatoum

Domesticities (bedframes, toys)
wired up and lethal,

nothing's for certain:
a cheese-grater divides a room;

light through
a wire cage casts

shadows, induces vertigo;
a propeller,

one blade furrowed,
the other straight,

makes a pattern
in sand, then erases it

Six works

1

are these fields
or a flatbed art
hemmed by mountains

these scatterings a sky
or a world above this one

a golden sunrise
a kneeling figure

ravines and temples
in clouds or speckled paint

2

a monstrous bird
on its side, beak
parting the black
collapsed caryatid
oblivious passer-by

3

the side of a silo
overcome by vegetation

4

an eye
or moon
in blue night

5

snow-melt
in the pastel's
upper corner

6

oil scraped off a landscape
the hill that fell off a wall

Hearsay

this office
this ventilator

'snipped into grabs'

piano bridge creek

peculiar atomism
lukewarm review

entrepôt
a knee itch

all that white
surrounds us

a fragile painting
without border

Toys

1

a doll's house
doors at the back
no apparent connection
between rooms
papered distinctively
small details, a bath,
a coal scuttle, figures
intent on their own activity
oblivious to each other
a collapsed wall
renders them public

2

a clockwork train
runs in a circle
between nowhere and nowhere else

3

a bear, a mouse and a bent dog
buried in a trunk
enter and leave the world as pathos

Hegemony

a world of transactions
at war with a world of immanence,
a geography without contours
against a range of singular spaces

a speech of sorts
lacks consequence, tied
to its own systole, diastole,
the rumble of traffic as contrabass

as though a carpet
were rolled up the neat lines
of buildings biographies
lurch to conclusion.

Lives of the Poets
[An edit from Journals, 1972-1983]

for Pam Brown

1

A sudden & brief thunderstorm over the house, the harbour.

A day in a car wash near Taylor Square.

Note on Brett Whiteley's Zen:
      all the detail is peripheral:
it was an easy step to bore a hole in the central panel & install a
light behind it.

I walk up the road to visit Terry Smith who is talking to a
friend whose husband has left suddenly so I accompany him
to the nearby milk bar near the Rowntree and Darling Street
intersection followed by Colin Talbot we run into Mia Pithie
who takes us to Robyn Ravlich's place and when she proves
absent to 'The Anchorage' which has been sold.

2

                  Cabramatta/light
                      an indescribable
                              (cerulean might be the word)
                                      blue

                  Liverpool:
          a rush at the kiosk for the *Daily Telegraph*

Cathy (Scorpio) & Pauline (Sagittarius?)
in the back, cases & cushions, *Guide to your Horoscope & Dreams*
(Library copy)

wrong turn thru Campbelltown
then back on 31 at Picton

Outskirts of Goulburn / Service station
'might be better to abandon it lady'
(a cracked bearing)

– guy in white ute
'used to work 7 days a week
have 4-5 months holiday
blow it all'

occasional WHIRR of car
yellow
almost silent
MONARO COUNTRY

Two trainee army officers
back from Rugby League to Wagga
'not much fuckin doin this
fuckin weekend'
(Psychology, German/& French: Sydney University)

car horn like a calf"s cry
lures cows from fields
(son of a farmer)

lift in a small yellow sports (drafty)
Monash Anthropology student w. long beard

golden sunset before Holbrook
half an apple.

Fire glow on a log
smoky car light over the rise

tantalised by Melbourne lights.
Flinders Street 10.15.
Suburbs (the 'Malvern house')

Clayton:
Allan Petersen & dog met in
the dark, Gentle Street.

3

it has an air of deja-vu,
an ease of execution:
it seems like a drawn out product of what precedes it

(thirteen loose pages of jottings)

'a great mulch, a great compost'

4

'I thought of the possibility of the last letter going astray.
Let me know if it has & I'll give you a breakdown of the New
Year trip.'

'I still haven't written anything and also am on the brink of
total bankruptcy which severely restricts my mobility. In order

to overcome this I've done & am doing a couple of odd jobs to supplement the dole which is often late in arriving & somewhat spasmodic. One job was a class at East Sydney Tech. I raved on poetry for the duration culling examples from O'Hara, Lew Welch, Jonathan Williams, Tranter, Allen Ginsberg & me (a found poem). I got the job almost accidentally when I was very stoned at a party the night before.'

'A house in the country may spell death, but at the moment I contemplate semi-permanent removal from the city with some degree of seriousness.'

5

rocks under the surface
the attempt to distance the actual from the fantasised,
                a transmutation

an alchemy renders rocks & stones
                into words
(a piece of music entitled
                'Quite early one morning')

                                (how does an 'object'
become notable – why separate a tree
from the air around it)

                Sugarloaf Creek poems
like Cold Mountain – a way of giving form
– but how true to its subject?

Han Shan writing on anything
                paper, wood, water – only the moment of interest

6

                              yesterday's ride through heavy rain
clearing at Armidale
        hanging round   waiting for a wheel balance
espresso in the Nectar milk bar

a long cloud bank stretched up & down the coast

the Putty road enveloped in deadness,
            then Colo, Windsor, Ryde,
                        the scene at Stuart's house
                some dope in the car,
                            a French restaurant

& this morning a letter from John Forbes in London

7

            Ballarat
            on an edge of basalt:
            the main street widens at this point

                        bend straws in the Chinese Cafe
            eat in a cold wind
                    Wendourie
            on the divide

Alan Wearne phones with polemical scherzo from Meredithian
sequence:
                    'fuck Diamond
                    fuck McKuen'

24

rain heavy, lightning more distant – in the single bed at 28 Eva
Street, the window part open.

8

      walk with Ken Bolton down Glebe Point Road,
a piece of paper blows towards us
            – it's part of the *Surfers' Paradise* reading poster
                – the lower part with feet of the surfer
Ken asks: 'Will our shit return to us in paperback?'

Fisher Library, 6th floor. stack.
Julie Rose working on her French MA thesis
me reading *Unspeakable Visions of The Individual*
                      #4/74
            THE BEAT BOOK
      on review for *Magic Sam* #3.

     it's dull & cold
out over Victoria Park   mowing lines,
swimming pool half full of dirty water
heavy traffic, City Road & Cleveland Street,
sky a medium grey, clear strip to the northwest.

finish reading M. Conrad Hyers
     Zen & the Comic Spirit

Interruption
          Denise Hare & Angela Korvisianos in the
courtyard cafeteria
someone passes a hash joint
& then I'm reading the last third of
     Whitman's 1855 preface

Home.
       finish a loaf of bread
glance through *Rolling Stone*
drink four cups of English Breakfast Tea
       wash the dishes
everyone's in the kitchen
       – I gotta get outa here –
(a place where conversation is like a novel of manners)

From unknown sources: 'Symbols, images, rhythmical perfection
… has never been considered as of primary importance by the
great poets, since refinement of form has often ended in triviality.'

&

'Kids get your Davy Crockett bed with scenes of Davy Crockett
in action on the mattress'

9

I live a primitive life in the city; know people who can wheel &
deal, do amazing things with tax forms. I simply barter my body
for money in terms of labour; make forays into the jungle to buy
trinkets & food.

       'What strikes me about many of the modern works in the
Art Gallery of New South Wales is that they have never *belonged*
anywhere though the category 'art' relates them somehow to the
Aboriginal and New Guinean artefacts downstairs in some kind
of cultural continuum. Martin Sharp's collection of fragments
from Luna Park has closer & deeper connections with its
surrounding culture than the works of the self-conscious artists.
       'The Gallery is a kind of nowhere living-room where grey

metal ashtrays sit half lost in white shaggy carpet around a chromium glass-topped table which never has anything on it. I look over a balustrade to see five men; one (the impatient one) not in a grey uniform, pacing back and forward while the others with the aid of a small fork-lift elevate a large Hans Heysen a certain number of centimetres from the floor.'

A big colour poster of Johnny Rotten under Steve Kelen's script: 'Annette Funicello's curse still grips Sydney'.

My poetry – a life watching curtains flutter.

10

Train down early Sunday morning to Coalcliff & a walk down to the beach while Ken & Sal Brereton put together posters & magazines for the evening. By 2 pm. a lot of people have arrived – Philip Hammial, Denis Gallagher, ΠO, Nigel Roberts, Phil Roberts & others. We go to Wollongong and the Al Monte. Phil Roberts delivers a paper called 'Death of the poet' then there's a break & the Wollongong writers read, Ken & Sal first, then another break followed by the Sydney contingent. Phil Roberts is interrupted by a Pyrmont anarchist whose child is playing with a soccer ball. Others read – Denis, ΠO (Mayakovsky & Nelson Algren & 'the fuck poems' shouted from a tabletop), John Tranter performs his 'Foucault at the Forest Lodge' pieces. A band play lounge music while everyone drinks & eats lukewarm lasagne.

I sleep in the pantry & wake early, the sun up over the ocean. A long breakfast turns into a picnic lunch in the back yard, then in the afternoon we go back into Wollongong to the Art Gallery (two coloured photos of Micky Allen's on display) & walk down to the beach – barbed wire & factories – tankers out on the Pacific.

11

> Very quiet, an occasional car sound.
> I've crossed some kind of meridian:
that bit in Williams' *Descent of Winter* where his pants feel 'strange upon a strange thigh'.

> It's grey out over the park,

these things come at once:
> winter, bad colds, the end of love.

Read Ted Berrigan's 'Sonnet LXXVI' ('It's my birthday').

> Dinner at Fort Street,

walk home in a break in the weather thinking grandiose thoughts about my poems.

12

Arrive late at Coalcliff, nobody about. Enter through a window and find *The Diamond Noodle* with a great picture of Philip Whalen on the back. Ken & Sal arrive half an hour before the train.

Coalcliff again, in time to help Ken re-affix the posts of the front verandah. Ken says he & Sal have split up. We walk halfway up

the mountain round the old track & then cut across a dip before
the final ascending stretch. At dusk we walk back past the cows
to the house imagining bad poems about this.

Strong winds sound like they'll blow the roof off.

Thirty pieces

for Angela Gardner

1

a suburb's
bars of light
on water where
once a blank
field a blanket
dark across
the river

2

purple horizon radiance
unnatural light the sweeping
ray of the airport red
wink of a landing plane

3

no need of
presence (anyone's)

4

they pass on, pass
it to you, who
don't know what to do

with it, make
a passable effort

5

the expert
lost in a moment
expertise, or lost
in a moment of expertise

6

the turtle beneath the elephant
stands on what?

7

newspapers turn history to pun

why concentrate at all
in this blue haze

8

the problem of agency

9

technology – not, finally, interesting,
its promotion in art a gambit

10

minimalism (not formalism)
– lighter
and deeper

11

temporary space

12

blue hills towards tambourine
the sign

and the seen

13

a col-
umn of
light the
river
warps
as wake

14

the density of air presses in, even in early April as though the
black were pigment massed about the skin. The orange lights
with not quite the clarity of the coming season

15

the knuckles white
of words bracing
about their task

16

to
and
fro
and
up
and
down

walking in Brisbane

17

a cross river ferry
intersects with an
upriver vessel
navigation lights
vanish behind
buildings

a world less rich
under these clouds

provisioned
from elsewhere

18

routines
stitched
together

energies
heavy
in air

19

a mass of tangled rope
a blocked out world of currents

20

the lamplight
of documents
your attention
stolen from coffee

21

the body as
endless surface

a figure eight

22

warm touch
(cold fingers)

integers

23

to
night

and to
morrow

24

the age of the end
of everything

25

incongruous
as a
gondola

26

animal noises
from the court

unseen fireworks
for what?

27

to take it to the edge of sense and then gently deposit it on the
bed of the mundane

28

the tape he sees
recording his voice
age six, gets
littler and littler

the voice heard now
says as much
before the click of spools

29

rain
avails

30

circumstance

a paper cup
in the river

One-Way Ticket

for Rosemary Hunter

what I have written
I have lost

what's recorded
so much paper and celluloid

the 1974 of desire moves
through its lack of movement

a moment
a memento

amen
a memory stick

a stack
of disks

a pile
of maps

*

worn down by detergents
I'm cleaner and smaller every day

*

the rain it raineth
on a dull tin roof

the anthologies arrive
the wars continue

mere anarchy
etcetera

3 a.m. (or 3 p.m.)
the worst times

death &
taxes

photocopies of everything

*

What I thought was Mo
was Osama Bin Laden
(the face on a half-tone poster)

so where is Stiffy?
(and who is *a friend of the groom?*)

*

spin & spam
vs. art, dust motes

that lightness, something
almost not there

those undeniable venetians
that would argue a pattern

a flying-fish
glued to the refrigerator

a space under the stairs
where memory sits

*

circular paths
a wrought-iron gate...

distant apartments
pipes, wind-vanes
funnels

walking figures
backwash
along the rocks

old military medals
account books
chess pieces
a tripod

electrical wiring

a stop watch
a slide-rule
mathematical tables

a microscope

calling cards

a red coat
on a green chair

the smell of fish
fresh marinaded

*

cut & paste:
a generation thing?
mine?   the beginnings
of insincerity?   embrace
of the artificial?

*

there's little sound
from down below

a mattock perhaps
at the edge of the pool

a moment to do nothing

bow wave of the ferry
slight aircraft noise

a chair is not a chair...

beached timber

smoke over Mt Gravatt

the tilers insert metal pegs
in the bottom of a wall

hammers echo across the river

already a heat haze at 8 a.m.

*

waves on the ceiling

tidal movements

*

an image of tired people in an airport lounge
painted by Michael Andrews:
The Last of Australia

coffee $3.25
black & white lines
dark wood

in the 33rd year &c (58th)
the body
within its limits

or without

*

be grateful for stairwells

for art at altitude

(a Martin Sharp playing card
circa 1980
in thanks for *East*,

a *tapa* print,

collapsing Cuban
tobacco barns

on a green slope

*

after the encomiums
a bouquet

an apartment of flowers

a fluttering screen

papers in bulk
letters I may never read again

a month before jacaranda season

*

points of light

shadows

gusts

a
lifting
floor

a
door

an orn-
ament

*

over the fold of the map

driving on the wrong side of the world

A northern winter

For Ken Bolton (who found it)

1

bitter gall in afternoon light
stroboscopic beech
'we will shortly be arriving at / Rainham'

a stationmaster spits the whistle

Tate Modern: Delaunay (Robert) and Severini, Munch and
Bonnard, Jonas Mekas' films. Gerhard Richter.

Before me (from the members' room), St Paul's and the Millennium Bridge. I will walk that way towards Lamb's Conduit (via
Shoe Lane, Holborn and Red Lion Streets), for Peter Riley and
Peter Philpott at The Lamb.

2

Today I sit downstairs in the office, looking out the back window
to our garage and wall and, above it, the last few yellow leaves
against a (rare) blue sky.

I see the sage plant beneath the window and immediately smell
(purely imaginary) sage.

3

What troubles me about Jackson Mac Low's methods is the mere thought of method. It seems essential that these works enunciate their principles of construction i.e. primary text, letter selection and secondary text. But is the knowledge of this supposed to bolster our appreciation of the result? If so are we admiring it because it fills the brief or are we admiring it for what it is? The two things are not necessarily compatible. MacLow realised at a certain point that there was no such thing as the purely aleatory, that the first principles were already an aesthetic decision.

4 *(Three musical interludes)*

i

Charlie Watts, dapper in Hatchards bookshop
a South London accent that may have been worked on

ii

in my head, the Horrie Dargie Quintet play
'East of the Sun and West of the Moon'

iii

I'd always hated Gary Shearston singing 'I get a kick out of you', but suddenly in the student bar, Roehampton, it all, especially the violinist, sounds good.

5

The snow from two nights back hasn't melted. Interesting to see which plants seem to have survived – lavender, thyme, oregano – that you might have expected to wilt. Tarragon dies off naturally, the rosemary hasn't really got going.

6

A white oblong of sun on the bedroom wall

Tonight, a reading in London which I'm not going to. That's three London events I'll have missed this week. Two because of weather, one, inertia.

7

nothing in *this* drawer

a tangle of script

'snowbound'

I feel less 'at home' here than I did a year ago. But would I feel 'at home' anywhere else?

8

If I have always envisaged work as music why do I still fear abandoning a patina of sense? The poems on the surface are 'documentary', but documents themselves don't 'last'. We don't read the poets (for the most part) for insights into the contemporary (though they ignore the past at their own peril).

9

speckled lights from Christmas
fake chandeliers

out there it's winter still
the bulbs in public gardens unopened

I decided today, walking through Canterbury, that what I feel now is a kind of blankness, a nothingness which seems neither bad nor good, neither exhilarating nor terrifying. It is maybe 'despond'. I need to emerge from it to write again, or if I write again I will emerge from it. I'm not certain which of these is true.

Now, I suppose, is the moment I stop being an observant tourist and become an ignorant local. Yet at the same time Australia appears an even odder construction. I mean I love it, aspects of it at least, but from here it's a peculiar thing. The fires that I know much about make it to the UK news, as does (as ever) 'shark attack'.

I belong to a space that nobody here will recognise.

10

spring bitter
and bitter spring
at The Sun

shadows on a page, the rise and fall of breath
striations in an enormous fireplace

marking time
marking, re-
marking

'Jim Thompson
never materialised
again'

11

The Fitzroy Tavern, Charlotte Street, last seen in, was it, 1992
or 1987? The 'writers and artists' bar is downstairs, but I stay
up, 'not writing', trying to remember the name of the Italian
restaurant I'm supposed to be at in half an hour.

telephones that ring like telephones

the ghost of Julian Maclaren-Ross shuffles past

'a violent hash smoker shakes a chocolate machine'

12

teasel
the burr of the plant, dried,
a device for carding wool

leaves that jump (dead ones) with a sound like raindrops
small greenish birds
an orange butterfly (fritillary?)

now I know the yew, found in churchyards, is poison to livestock

13

and now it's daylight saving

when will the scaffolding come down?

and what place for *this* scaffold
in the age of interruption?

miniature daffodils under the tarpaulin
a sign ('The Sun') on its side;
inside, from the rafters,
hops, still green from summer

New York Notes

for Basil & Martha King

1

legs of a shop dummy
protrude from a junkpile
dusted with snow

2

sunlight on warehouse roofs and cinder pits
dull shade of ice on a canal

3

pond light flickers over
hung saucepans, a worn rug

4

at the Cloisters, medieval plunder,
the Palisades and Paterson across the river

frozen waterfalls on rock

a unicorn fenced in a circle

5

on Coney Island
a silent boardwalk

Postcards from Massachusetts

for Jess Mynes & Ruth Lepson

1
dun home counties sky

2
aloft, between Porcupine Bank
and the Charlie Gibbs Fracture Zone

3
under Orion (O'Ryan)
50 miles from Gloucester

traceries in Lincoln's night air
pine needles on the skylight

4
an orientation speaker with irritating voice
traverses Harvard Square, as I arrange poems
on the steps of the church

5
air-conditioning blasts the curtains,
an orange crane swings south,

Bunker Hill viewed at an angle,
the Charles River over there

I keep thinking 'Dirty Water'

6
turn up the heat and order in

7
Concord is 'conquered'
rail trucks overgrown in a siding

Amherst, Ms Dickinson's house,
her grave, back of seventies shops

8
reading at the café-bar in Wendell
I find myself 'leaning on the john door'

9
I feel like the English character in an American movie:
'I've really had a jolly good time thank you'

10
tailback at Concord roundabout

no rest from this condensery

11
everywhere's a building site
this whole part of Boston is money

the coastguard slips out
by the Institute of Contemporary Art

12
PARADISE SELF-STORAGE
near Swampscott, where Eigner
looked out on the street from a glazed porch

then Salem in angled sunlight,
at Gloucester The Cut,
tyre rumble on Blynman Bridge

this republic (and its Republicans)
viewed in gloom
from Half-Moon Beach

13
bagel parlour talk:
'why did they axe *you*?'

14
Halloween's een
a dark blue sky behind apartments
thinned out yellow leaves foreground

and then Paul Kelly in the foyer:
'have you ever seen Sydney from a 727 at night?'

15
Logan: the Durgin-Park Bar
'established before you were born'

candidate Scott Brown's fake tears, and
'now the Panthers have their first
give-away for the night'

16
the torn edges of both continental shelves,
suddenly a horizon,

somewhere down there, a disused shed
in Co. Wexford

17
on Southeast Rail
the voice of England: 'All our toilets
are in working order this morning'

Changi

for Chris Kelen

three young men watch movies on their phones
one snorts loudly

SHOP & REDEEM   ANGRY BIRDS™
SPACE PLUSH

sculptural objects, glass boxes
an atrium of indoor palms

Xmas muzak, a large (tour?) group
a safari suit (thought extinct),

'so far and no safari', said Mark
(to Philip Whalen in Heaven)

DO NOT OBSTRUCT
FIREMAN ACCESS PANEL

'what me worry?!'
about the price of krill?

Territorial

clouds and the shadow of clouds,
dry watercourses, tincture of metal

Lake Eyre white
with blue shadows

Gloria Petyarre's ridges
purple and yellow

Adelaide

things in cold places
a hemisphere away

here, a flicker
of light on a hat stand,

brightness, beyond a dark hall,
late November

a sheoak squared
in a screen door

the state bird singing
in the gums

After a storm, Brisbane

the forest reclaims the street

frangipani
         & gecko

early currawongs   noisy miners

a corrugated iron roof stretches

dead leaves on a flowering tree
might be flying foxes:
one patch moves, counter to the wind

spaces contract
spoons clink in the neighbours' breakfast bowls

a man in overalls appears to fix something
up outside steps a block away

An ordinary evening in Newtown

For Stephen Muecke

1

Camperdown's for dogs,
Friday evening in the park off Church Street

a barefoot man
carries a plank:
                              it's like
La Grande Jatte
for airedales
                    under the flight path

2

a square-faced guy
underpants protruding from his jeans
in the smoky atmosphere of the Court House

the word HOT, above the wood roof of the outside bar
(neon in daylight)

'are you fuckin married or what!?'

3

in the Carlisle Castle 'Crimson & Clover',
the forty-somethings

(Church t-shirt,
dingo before pyramid)

vivid pink drinks,
a faint vomit smell from the kitchen (cheese?)

and now, the meat raffle

Sideways Café

for David Musgrave

traverse property,
a bowling club, apartment block,
then walk up Union

approaching people resolve into strangers
the breeze drops briefly

eastern rosellas in flight
drawn across the pages of a book
as if by tab
                              (there's
a Frank Gehry
pop-up, but

how hard is it
to fold the buildings back?)

Differant curioes

for Jann Chambers & Greg Maguire

once you could see the trains from this yard
now it's a forest,

Illawarra flame in the canopy,
magpie lark on the floor

someone sings from the adjoining flats

*

a geography: gullies
empty into Botany Bay via Cook's River, Wolli Creek

the bay now largely clean,
at La Perouse white beaches,

a former snake pit,
a fenced-off church

a laneway in Pyrmont called Cadigal

*

words slide around in their possible configurations
a concatenation of rail trucks parse the sentence
as idle leaves droop

how much weight does a tree invest in dead branches?

Sydney moisture: at once cold and hot
densities of air
                    undergrowth of text

I read the small print of album covers

*

this room in half-light
of paintings 'by various hands'

the objects in Ken Searle's work: louvered window, tiny corner of
red-yellow cloth in another distant opening; foreground: paint
peeling off the edge of a table, red and yellow handle of a kitchen
utensil (an echo)

the brown bottle appears concave

*

spanish moss above wrought iron leaves

a shadow of clothing on the grass

Northcote

for Jeanette Hoorn & Barbara Creed

cool breeze through pink and yellow eucalypts
as trains hiss into Westgarth station

a possible honk of geese or ducks
from the Merri Creek

warm air in a cool house
three kookaburras aligned on tea canisters,

art deco cups and saucers,
a Roman face, Minerva, above acanthus

strands of pollen fallen on white paper
meniscus of water round garden pots

a loose screw from somewhere,
rusted, thread intact

Williamstown

for Sarah Biddulph & David MacInnes

1

low native scrub on the promontory
palm-ends splattered with birdshit

upper decks of ships
luminous in the Bay

cloud from the northeast gathers,
the poems dry up,

at the edge of the military base, leaves hang
awaiting scent release

the closest gum, a scribbly trunk,
red-tipped branches,

amid the foliage, bunches
of spherical green pods

2

turbulence on Port Phillip,
Hobson's Bay out of sight, behind the station,
Corio behind the football stands

anamometers spin

three khaki trucks
two yellow outboards

```
KEEP CLEAR
HEAVY LOADING &
UNLOADING USE ONLY
```

cirrostratus as punctuation

3

rusted locks face south and east

only the upper level cognisant of light

the rail draped with spiderwebs

a loose strip of flywire

fur jacket on a collapsed settee

The Oxford Book of Jurisprudence

4

a kite, bird-shaped
above the depot

above a protected cove
of black swans

vessels silhouetted
seaward.

the brilliant device
perturbs local birds

hovering low
over the parade ground

an asphalt park's
empty space,

wire fence disappears
over a hump, on which

the great one falls
entangled on barbs.

over the battery
gulls rejoice

the raptor, unpicked
lifts off, then plummets

gains altitude again,
then it's gone

5

low coastal eucalypts, ti-tree, palms (introduced)
bend with the wind

figures leave the park
waves flatten

lights, port side
of a monolith

shades of grey-blue
above and below

an odd chromaticism
ship shape under cloud

chatter of settled birds
upstairs, under billiard lights

Goodbye Ava Gardner

for Cameron Lowe & Tim Wright

Fly in from the east, the Ninety-Mile,
mud islands off Wilson's Promontory,
                                    to this place
of long cool terraces, fanlight
over front door, a gap beneath,

these wide streets, their median strips
broad enough for picnics,

an occasional breeze
from Hobson's Bay

this corner of the city

*

The Age hits the porch

cloud, west beyond the chimneys, masses,
hints a storm

someone practices bass
I read the street directory

white roses, red geraniums,
a backyard otherwise bare

a mess in the street
now gone (Amess Street)
bar the boxes

*

                            'almost all of Melbourne was there'
if not in Italy
at least in Lygon Street,
                   the Università
where the old Italian boss takes our photograph,
pretends to pocket the camera and run
                            (an old joke
but he does it well)

was that a tram
or the sound of rain approaching?

*

the space of this inner suburb is all sky,
a ridge down to Carlton
                    (from Elgin Street, the dip then, distant,
those childhood mountains
                    the Dandenongs

*

all those years of illegible script
(notebooks from this city date back to sixty-eight)
the scribble dilates,
                   odd moments comprehensible

a blackbird (female) scrounges through bark chips,
part of what looks like a ruined pediment,
a head, maybe, like the robot in Ken's backyard
                    'look on me ye mortals...' &c

all this under the shrub rose, the wrought iron lattice,
the open garage, its shelves of bags containing other bags

peculiar austerities of other people

*

the superimposition of pattern is African:
Japanese fabric under a check picnic rug
on a 1970s sofa; stripes against animal shapes;
a Persian and an Afghan carpet

then I make a milk run to the Vietnamese grocer

*

the pen runs out
(as the toothpaste, the shaving cream)

adjust to leaving here
                              'the last place on earth'
once a movie with
a bored female lead

we chase the dark
across the map
                              'blizzards in Britain'

diagrammatic dunes west of Muscat,
a miniature sun above the Queensland coast

and hours to go before I sleep

Dogs, part whatever

Life on Mars

'Am I a light bulb?'
                    – tortured Iraqi

No, my friend, you're an
'electric pear'

*

Things to do in East Kent, Parts 1, 2 & 3

1
listen to Soft Machine
'We did it again'

2
listen to Soft Machine
'We did it again'

3
listen to Soft Machine
'We did it again'

*

OLD HAT SPEAKS!

*

a fine day in
the decline of the west

*

a plaster dog and cat
chained to the shopfront
of the RSPCA

*

After Pete Brown

I stumbled into the john
in the John Curtin
and saw, written
on the tiles 'John
Forbes is fucking awesome'

*

Is Duchamp's Large Glass
half full or half empty?

*

the new avant are touchy
like movie stars

*

Barcode   *for Alan Halsey*

if it's not a free country
at least it's a free house

*

Australiana #2

a large mulga snake met an untimely death after getting its head
stuck in an empty beer can

*

The Ghost of WCW in a Faversham Pub

'I'd love to go back
to Acapulco

it was so different
and so easy'

*

A Jonathan Williams moment in Hay-on-Wye

GIANT BOOK SALE
at Three Cocks

*

The Art of Poetry

don't write when you have 'something to say'
write when you have nothing to say

*

Snow

the air almost makes it exist,
incipient, imminent, if not present

*

After Harvey Shapiro

I read the Hebrew 'bereshit'
as 'bear shit'.
In the beginning was the bear.

*

smaller than the syllable:
the Silliman

*

Universal Toilet

this train has,
says the 'onboard manager',
a 'universal toilet'

*

do horses dream
of hamburgers?

*

in the middle of the poem
the sound downstairs of drunks
singing Happy Birthday

*

Tragedy

the body of an immense teddy bear
balanced on a hedge

*

Editorial

this is the age of the fat cheque
not the fact check

*

Mime

figures on a rooftop
silently perform
in advance of the storm

*

Mere Anarchy

in a hutch on Faversham Station
an overweight worker smokes a pipe

*

Redaction

My heart is in my pocket.
It is a tiny photograph of
Ron Padgett's *Collected Poems*

*

dans le restaurant the poet
awaiting a slow bill
texts his absence from the seminar

*

Heritage   *for John James*

Inside Wales there is a small place called Wales

*

In the City

at five the suits appear,
the boisterous camaraderie

'glorious 2012' it says
on the tap

*

Terza Rima

Vegetarian = V
GF = gluten-free
prices include VAT

*

'with the hint of summer
our minds turn to salad'

*

the anti-fun
antiphon

*

Address

High Dudgeon, Kent

*

the shop that sold pink cakes
sells e-cigarettes

the shop that sold nothing in particular
sells nothing at all

*

at Seven Dials: 'psychic readings –
appointments not always necessary'

*

Imperative

choose the burger

*

Surf's up

'Pipeline' (the Chantays), then
'Bombora', didn't indicate this future:
rain on the stones of Whitstable beach

*

Georgia

The sun sets behind the little church, but lights are on in the big house. Below the cliffs two men on a raft have nearly finished eating a table of fish while two more display a leg of ham, seemingly hauled from the depths. There is a symbol painted on the cliff behind them which they do not seem to notice. It is the most important thing in this picture.

*

A Slim Volume

The Cambridge Book of Post-Avant Comic Verse

*

Shambolism: a manifesto

'If it looks like a shambles, it probably is'

*

The Louis Jordan/WCW mash up

there ain't
nobody here

but us
white chickens

*

A Shropshire Lad

Much Wenlock
about nothing

After Gael Turnbull

The gales are battering the trees.
The broadband signal's breaking up.
Cam says no to refugees.
Will Andy win the Davis Cup?

There'll be flooding on the levels.
Buy a ticket, scratch and see.
The SNP are bloody devils.
Labour's under Jeremy.

Scotland's fallen off the map.
The First Great Western's running late.
The EU is a load of crap.
It's Faber, so it *must* be great.

An Excursion and a Visit

i.m. Lee Harwood

a cellphone photograph
(blurred) of Chanctonbury Ring
up from Buncton chapel, 2007

trees mark the site, partly flattened
by gales twenty years back, resuming a shape,

a semblance of high wind,
clouds massing, the profile of a hilltop.

a mechanical duck pedals a tricycle
across a floor in Hove,

the sea down the road
a limit horizon (described as a wall
                    by Paul Evans

a ruined pier
rusted metal flutings

                    the Regency had time
for such amusements

Reflections on his sixty-seventh year

a whole month,
so far and no safari
(a glasses case but no glasses –
I can write but can't read)

fluttery chest, bung knee, Spitfire Gold

earlier, in Canterbury, a cloud of seagulls,
books about Dijon and Burgundy,
maps of Ironbridge, Much Wenlock

the daffodils haven't flowered,
all other plants unseasonal,

frost burnt off the jasmine,
a fat pigeon crushed the ground cover

so many buildings in this neighbourhood
boarded (or papered) up

Bad Pennies, Bad Pandas (bands)

'ullo … ullo … ullo …'
a phone natterer, loud, partly deaf –
her companion half-asleep over a pint

the old people wear jeans these days
('we wear jeans')

the young wear shorts

Autumn Journal

gulls caught in early light over rooftops

yellow sky

*

one red fox, several deer

the length of the King's Wood

*

mud and twigs

cracked acorns on a wet road

*

the steep descent from Soakham Downs

a groove filled with mulch

*

cross-hatched hillside

at Warren Farm

*

smoke turns to fog

moonrise south of Gravesend

*

rough winds

wrong equinox

At Glasbury

for John Goodby & Lyndon Davies

above the slates a wall of foliage
hit by sunlight, the Black Mountains
pale green in a hailstorm

behind me a half-collapsed iron structure,
a kitchen garden, then open field and the braided Wye

upper surfaces of cumulous clouds protrude from the high fields
then pale blue, a sky
reputedly full of stars

on the road:
ARAF

in the bar:
𝔪𝔦𝔫𝔡 𝔶𝔬𝔲𝔯 𝔥𝔢𝔞𝔡

'this is the closest thing to crazy
I have ever been
I'm 22
and I'm acting 17'

then

Moonlight Serenade played on a Butlin's Hammond

The Gorge

Under an iron footbridge,
the Severn's quiet,

dead branches testify to flood,
river heights marked

on the door of The Ship,
by now uninsurable.

A bank of trees hides the slope
to Madeley, 'a Victorian village'.

Nobody makes things here anymore.

Mitchell's Fold

From White Grit
a farm road

then moorland,
a broken circle of stones.

Two joggers approach,
navigate the site

as though touch
could transfer energy,

otherwise: silence.
Wales is blue haze,

a kite hangs
above the border

Town & Gown

for Simon Smith, Ben Hickman & Kat Peddie

Is there room in the room…
there's breeze in the yard
after the poets in RX 11

waiting for the 23.02
T-shirt weather

'I'd rather have a couple of drinks and get drunk'

'He fancies you'

'I'd rather fuckin get drunk'

Alight here for the Cathedral and University

'Part of Bristol is still rich'

A fat man in immense jeans, too big for his legs
(not his waist) breasts the bar

I hear the word 'schooner'. Is this local?

Baseball cap and waxed moustache shifts the drinks;
in a glass box, a wooden vat, a steel vat; tiles
a bilious green.

Outside: wind off the Atlantic
almost blows my hat off;

the colour of those Georgians on the crest of a hill;
slave ships on the river.

A short history of France

for Jane Zemiro

In Toulouse winged beasts
line the courtyard of an old convent,

there's a room of Romanesque capitals,
large paintings of wars

fought elsewhere, mountains
closer than they are now.

The last city defences
demolished 1820,

red brick channels
the Garonne's rapids,

trees snagged on rocks
from a recent flood.

Movement of wind through plane leaves
is pointillisme.

In the riverside bar a student reads
One Dimensional Man.

Angers sur Maine

for Ian Brinton

There was once a fun-fair on this site –
a photo from the 1920s shows *l'auto tamponnaise*

across the city Babylon collapses,
frogs in the mouths of inhabitants,

fire, flood & locusts –
the fourteenth century knew this.

Under an old church
stone coffins radiate about a well,

north of the river a thunderstorm threatens.
We find an African bar. End up in a Japanese restaurant.

L'Helice Terrestre

For Tony Baker & Liz Hanaway

an 'earth propeller'
gouged from limestone

soft, damp, chalklike
a place bands could play in

if it all came to nothing,
the surface transformed

as in Lurçat's cosmos
to dust and stars

in this placid *department*
known for its wine

its villages built on the levee
of a fast-running river

A bridge

steps

pockets of colour

vermilion on the far side

an escalator uphill

Pessoa (bronze)

sits outside the café

Da Silva's splinters of light depict

a city of depth and distance

the wings of a butterfly   *borboletta*

dry underleaf

in a run-down garden

broad harbour beyond the Praça do Comércio

a climate   blown eastward

under the bridge called April 25th

Vedute

Palermo

It could be out of Francesco Guardi
this city, though he was Venetian,

these buildings with grassy pediments,
everything run down

hinting at greatness, then
masking it with concrete.

In the Villa Giulia by the central fountain
the busts have mostly lost their heads.

Cats doze in the Orto Botanico
between potted succulents; the dogs,

stray but docile,
sleep on the footpaths

*

Demolition

A square of houses, windows bricked in.
Around these, dust, gamblers, the edge of a market.

A block away streets resume their regular pattern

*

Items

Mario Sironi's grey street, 1920,
a small truck, blocked
by tram number 304,

a hint of the traffic outside now;
Renato Guttuso's nude, made of
newspaper; these

in the Galleria d'Arte Moderna.
In the Galleria Regionale
Antonello da Messina's Madonna,

the head of Eleanora of Aragon
by Francesco Laurana,
smooth enough for a later century.

Outside in the courtyard
an attendant, snaps off as gifts
cuttings of aromatic plants.

*

Baroque

The baroque was always an add-on:
facades tell of uncertain gravity,

painted ceilings,
features 'to pass out under',

the Battle of Lepanto in gold on white plaster,
something to take the breath away

*

Catacombs

They grin or howl,
heads twisted from bodies

each hangs forward
unsupported by neck muscle

some in bow ties
some in moth-eaten trousers

those in the professions
have their own aisles

those of the cloth
the darkest spaces

all are covered
by thick dust

*

Contours

After Termini
the train cuts inland

up a river valley
towards a divide;

market gardens
give way to dry country,

eucalypts, referred to
by Lampedusa,

olives
and prickly pear,

uplands, ploughed
within an inch of erosion,

precipitous rocks: signs
of slippage,

boulders, break the flow
in ravines; above,

a village, Sutera,
circumnavigates a peak.

*

Agrigento

The cathedral threatens collapse,
a shoulder of the hill northward

prone to subsidence. The steps before it
fenced off, contain

running shoes filled with concrete.
The ruins are a few miles out,

Africa a little further.

Notes

As the title implies this is an unholy gathering of discrete pieces written over the last fifteen years. There are quite a few '747 poems' here: things written in transit that I hope escape their circumstances enough to be of amusement. When I started to write poems I often omitted to dedicate them to the various friends who had often enough occasioned them. This time around I've hopefully been more generous, helped along by the sense that poems, for the most part, are parts of a conversation and, in that respect, are inherently occasional. 'One Way Ticket' mentions Stiffy and Mo, two Australian 'blue' comedians of the thirties. The 'friend of the groom' references a poem by Paul Blackburn, 'Night Cappy'. 'Differant Curioes' takes its misspelt title from a line in Kenneth Slessor's poem 'Five Bells'. 'Goodbye Ava Gardner' refers to the actress who felt, while filming Neville Shute's *On The Beach* (1959), that Melbourne was an appropriate place to make a movie about the end of the world. 'After Gael Turnbull' is a 2015 take of Gael's 1957 poem 'Now that April's here'. Both poems are about received wisdoms. 'L'Helice Terrestre' refers to Jacques Warminsky's underground sculptural-site-as-dwelling in the Loire valley. Tony Baker assures me that bands (including his and Liz Hanaway's) have played there. 'Lives of the Poets' is an excavation from early journals. In 'Reflections on his sixty-seventh year' the line 'we wear jeans' comes from an early work by Ken Bolton, 'poem, the terrific days of summer'. 'A northern winter' was rescued from a file I'd sent to Ken in 2009 and promptly forgotten. Until now many of these pieces had, as Chuck Berry said, 'no particular place to go'.

Acknowledgements

Thanks to the editors of all these publications:

For One Boston (edited by William Corbett), *Best Australian Poems 2013* (edited by Lisa Gorton), *To This Quiet Spot: University of Reading Creative Arts Anthology 2013* (edited by Kirsty Hambrook), *A Festschrift for Tony Frazer* (edited by Richard Berengarten, Aidan Semmens & others), *Best Australian Poems 2016* (edited by Sarah Holland-Batt).

Australian Book Review, *Cordite* (Australia), *flash cove* (Australia), *Great Works* (UK), *The Harvard Review* (USA), *Journal of Poetics Research* (Australia), *Molly Bloom* (UK), *Noon* (Japan), *otoliths* (Australia), *Plumwood Mountain* (Australia), *Poetry International* (Netherlands), *Port* (USA), *Shampoo* (USA), *Southerly* (Australia), *Splinter* (UK), *Stride* (UK), *Stylus* (Australia), *Sure Hope* (UK), *Tears in the Fence* (UK), *The Wonderbook of Poetry* (Macau), *Zone* (UK)

'After Gael Turnbull' and 'The Louis Jordan/WCW mash up' appeared on my blog, Graveney Marsh. 'Thirty Pieces' and 'One-Way Ticket' first appeared in the limited edition book *Leaving Here*, published by Angela Gardner's Light-Trap Press in Brisbane, 2012 (Angela, I owe you one).

And thanks, as ever, to Rosemary Hunter.

www.ingramcontent.com/pod-product-compliance
Lightning Source LLC
Chambersburg PA
CBHW022159080426
42734CB00006B/500